I0539118

For my kids: Isabella, Michael, and Danny.
Please take these lessons seriously in the future
in case I am not around to sit down with you
at our kitchen table and teach you myself. I
truly believe they can change your lives.

"Life is like a parachute jump; you've got to get it right the first time."

–Eleanor Roosevelt

10 THINGS NOBODY TOLD ME ABOUT MONEY

LIFE LESSONS ABOUT BUILDING WEALTH EVERYONE SHOULD KNOW AND TEACH THEIR KIDS

BRAD WIEHER

Murphy Publishing House

© 2025 Brad Wieher

All rights reserved. This book or any portion thereof may not be reproduced or used in any manner whatsoever without the express written permission of the publisher except for the use of brief quotations.

Interior design by Taryn Nergaard
Cover design by Kristen Paige Andrews

ISBN 979-8-218-66404-6 (Paperback)
ISBN 979-8-218-64183-2 (eBook)

CONTENTS

INTRODUCTION

I am going to tell you something that you need to hear before it's too late: Every single one of you has the power to build wealth and become a millionaire. A superpower, even.

However, your superpower isn't unlimited strength, lightning speed, or invincibility. Your superpower is time, and, strangely enough, your kryptonite is also time. Time can make you rich, and it can keep you poor—and it doesn't care. It also never stops ticking, and it won't rewind, no matter how hard you try. So listen up and take what I am about to tell you very seriously: There are no do-overs. No second chances. No time machines (that I am aware of, at least).

Think about this: if you *could* go back in time, knowing what you know now about life and about money, what would you tell yourself? Is there anything you would do differently a second time around? To be clear, I'm not talking about sharing secret futuristic knowledge about investments that hit it big, or passing off Biff's Sports Almanac with a note to watch out for Marty McFly. What I am talking about is that looking back, the truth has always been pretty simple. Had we all known more about how money works when we were young and acted on that knowledge, many of us would be millionaires today.

It's hard to wrap my head around even now at age 42, how truly simple it all really was (and still is), and the scary part is that it wouldn't have taken a superpower to do it. It would have taken financial guidance from someone around us when we were young, and it would have taken consistency, and belief, and time. That's it!

The truth is, having knowledge about how money works and how it grows and compounds over time when invested, especially at a young age, does in fact give you a superpower after all. It is the power to see the future with such simplicity and such clarity that you *know,* and I mean *know,* based on mathematical certainty, that the financial future you envision today can and will come true if you follow a simple plan. And so you do. And so one day it does.

Had we all known at a young age how simple building wealth could be, we would have started saving and budgeting and investing sooner and more regularly than many of us did. We would have begun funding our children's college saving plans sooner too. Like the day after they were born (joking, but not really). We would have stayed away from high-interest credit cards and debt, left the thirty-year mortgages on the curb, and saved up for that slightly used car and paid cash. We would have started a vacation fund long before any vacation. Started an emergency fund before any emergency. Started a retirement fund. Started a Christmas fund?

If given the chance to jump into a time machine and start again, the list goes on. Not because we did anything wrong necessarily, but simply because we were young and just didn't know any better. Or we didn't listen. Or both.

The truth is, we all didn't have someone sitting at the kitchen table with us guiding each financial step of the way. Showing us how to open tax-free college savings plans for our children and reminding us how important it is to fund them while they are young. Then reminding us again and again when we got busy and "life happened" and our investments took a back seat.

Someone pushing us to start saving up cash for that car long before it was needed and explaining to us why. I mean, really, why? We have good jobs now, careers even, and can afford the monthly payments when the time comes. And what's a sinking fund, anyway?

Sure, you can qualify for a loan and buy that big house, but should you? Would a little less house with a little more elbow grease and a fifteen-year mortgage be good enough for now and smarter financially in the long run?

These are conversations many of us just didn't have when we were young. Not because we didn't have great parents or an awesome family or good friends—I honestly did and still do—, but because we just didn't talk about money in that way. Many of us still don't. If that sounds familiar, congratulations: you're normal.

We didn't know how much money our parents made, how much money was in the bank, or how it was being invested or saved or for what purpose. We didn't discuss how they handled student loans or the dangers of debt.

We didn't know their long-term retirement strategy or the reasoning behind it. We didn't know if they had life insurance. Our parents didn't talk about that with us, likely because their parents didn't talk about it with them. It just was how it was, and we didn't think much about it. We chalked it up to "a more private generation" so "mind your own business, kid."

However, that also left many of us out there learning as we went. Just L.I.V.I.N.' (Matthew McConaughey reference, anyone?) when we were young and doing the best we could with what we knew about money at the time, which quite honestly wasn't as much as we thought.

My wife, Jill, and I had three babies under the age of two years old when we were in our late-twenties. Yes, our daughter was less than two years old when BAM!, we were blessed with twins, and identical twin boys at that!

We were thinking about how to keep the boys from climbing the cabinets and swinging from the chandeliers and how to keep their older sister from riding the dogs around the house like wild horses while wearing a princess tiara and waving a blue magic wand. We were wondering things like, *did we buy enough diapers? Where are the diapers? Why is the diaper on his head and not on his butt? Did we shower this week?* We were outnumbered, and although we were having the best time, we were also in survival mode, whether we knew it or not. College for them was so many years away. I couldn't even imagine. There would be plenty of time to save. Or so we thought.

Where were the financial TikTok experts talking about investing and compound interest and high yield savings accounts when we were young? Where were the financial radio shows and the witty podcasts? Where were the older and wiser who had lived and learned? Not cool for living and learning and not teaching us.

Why didn't someone step in and teach all of us how to live a debt-free life when we were kids? How to save, and invest, and become wealthy over time in a society overflowing with credit cards and debt. Why wasn't this taught in school? These were the lessons we all needed!

So many big decisions in life are happening while we are young. Decisions that continue to ripple across the rest of our lives. A thirty-year mortgage? No problem! "You can afford the monthly payment and have been approved for the loan," said every mortgage loan officer ever. House poor? What's house poor? With steady raises year over year, unfailing health, and never-ending good fortune, the next three-hundred and sixty monthly payments over the next 30 years of your life will be more than affordable!

How about that first car purchase—or two? No problem, it's only seventy-two easy $500 monthly payments at 6 percent interest for the next 6 years! Where do we sign?

How about that credit card debt? Going to pay the balance off every month, huh? Sounds like a plan! Hope the points and airline miles are worth the risk of going into debt. Any "no payments for six years at 0 percent interest" purchases these days? After all, you bought that big new house and have to furnish it. How about those school loans? Still waiting for the government to forgive them? How about saving for retirement? Kids going to college someday? Thought about life insurance? Yikes.

Can you imagine how many people today are worried about their retirement? Secretly scared they may never be able to retire comfortably because they began saving and investing "too late" and, you know, inflation. We all know perfectly well that wealth-building compounds over the years and, make no mistake, most of us need those years. That time plus consistency of investing is the unstoppable flywheel.

Start young, invest 15 percent of your income, and let it

grow and compound year over year. Time simply cannot be made up without large sums of money, which would not have been needed if you began investing in mutual funds and funding your retirement accounts regularly early on. Unfortunately, before many of us even knew to.

Here is something to think about: If you invest $500 per month from age twenty-five to age sixty-five, you will have around $3,000,000 (3 million dollars!) when you retire, assuming an average rate of return of around 10 percent over those years. You will be a multi-million-aire, and we know this mathematically based on the average rate of return in the stock market over the last one hundred years. However, wait fifteen years and start investing the same $500 per month from age forty to age sixty-five, and you will have around $600,000. Roughly 2.5 million dollars less.

Now don't get me wrong, $600,000 is still a lot of money, and do start investing at age forty if you have not already. It's never too late to do the right thing, and when we know better we do better, but ouch! What a difference time makes. Sorry, there are no "do-overs" on that one.

So why didn't we all do it right the first time when we

were young? Well, I don't know about you, but nobody sat me down at the kitchen table at age fifteen, looked me in the eye, and taught me what they spent their entire lifetime learning the hard way about money. And at least back then, if that didn't happen, we had to figure it out for ourselves. We didn't have Facebook and YouTube and TikTok videos (as mathematically incorrect as many of them are) to learn from if we were so inclined, and likely at that age, we were not.

So here is what I am going to do. I am going to do for you what I truly wish someone had done for me. I am going to teach you myself.

I hope these lessons make a big difference in your life, no matter your age or financial situation. Read these stories with your teenagers if you're a parent, read them on your own if you're on your own, read them with young families just starting out, read them with your church group, read them at work, read them in class at school, read them with anyone you think they might be able to help. That is what I am going to do with my kids when the time comes, and that is what I hope you do too.

Mark Twain once said that writers should write what

they know. Well, I wrote what I needed to know and what I think many people today may still need to know too. Possibly, more than ever.

Here it goes.

10 THINGS NOBODY TOLD ME ABOUT MONEY

Life Lessons about Building Wealth Everyone Should Know and Teach Their Kids

1. Monthly Budgets Make Millionaires. It All Starts Here.

2. Start Saving and Investing Right Now. I Promise You, It's Time.

3. Begin Investing Long-Term for Your Retirement. Like Right Now.

4. Credit Cards Build Credit Scores, and Debt, Not Wealth. If You Can't Afford to Pay Cash for It, You Can't Afford It.

5. Large Monthly Car Payments Don't Make Millionaires. Pay Yourself, Not the Bank.

6. Fifteen-Year Home Mortgages or Nothing. No Exceptions. This Is a Big One.

7. Open a 529 College Savings Plan for Each of Your Kids and Begin Funding Them Monthly. No Matter How Small the Amount.

8. Buy Life Insurance for You and Your Spouse the Minute You Have a Family That Is Counting on You. Trust Me.

9. Life Is Expensive and Getting More Expensive. Find a Side Hustle.

10. Carry Cash, Be Generous, and Stay Focused Out There. Money isn't Money. It's Freedom.

Lesson 1

MONTHLY BUDGETS MAKE MILLIONAIRES.
IT ALL STARTS HERE.

"You can make money two ways,
make more or spend less."

- John Hope Bryant

"Do not save what is left after spending,
but spend what is left after saving."

- Warren Buffett

"The art is not in making money, but keeping it."

- Proverb

LESSON 1

One thing is for sure, if you are trying to build wealth, you need to spend less money than you make, and the only way to know what is happening for sure is to set a monthly budget.

It doesn't matter if you are twenty-five years old and single, just starting out with a young family, forty-five years old with kids moving towards college, or if you are retired. If you don't have a monthly budget, now is the time to start one. Like right now. So hurry up and read this chapter.

Oh, and did I mention that this is going to be fun? Yes, understanding your finances can be a lot of work, and, yes, it takes time and consistency, but make no mistake, it's fun!

You work too hard day in and day out to not know where your money is going each month and to not have a clear plan for how every dollar will be spent, saved, or invested.

Now, don't expect your budget to be perfect right away. Most people take a few months to adjust their budgets here and there and really start to lock in and tighten up their expenses around month three. For now, the important part is that you have one.

Also, don't expect all months to be the same. Some months are just different and cost more, like December. Your December budget should not necessarily look like your June budget. Most people expect to spend more money in December, and, if that is the case, they should plan ahead and budget for that. I mean, Christmas is expensive and in December each year as far as I know!

Let's look at a sample budget together, and, just for fun, let's look at the difference between a budget that includes monthly credit card payments versus one without any consumer debt payments (any debt besides the home mortgage) while using the same combined household income of $10,000 per month for both. Did I mention yet how important it is to stay away from credit cards?

Now, in real life, all household budgets will look different based on so many factors. Combined household monthly income, number of kids in the home, personal and professional goals, amount of debt, mortgage payment amount, number of pets, sports, hobbies, taxes, etc.

At the same time, many utility line items are similar across most households such as gas, electricity, internet, water, and so on. They may not cost the same for everyone, but these are bills most of us have and pay for monthly regardless of how much money we make or where we live.

Let's take a look at a sample budget for a family of five (2 parents, 2 dogs, and 3 teenagers who are active in sports).

Example Family Budget 1: $10,000/Month - Contains Consumer Debt Payments

BUDGET ITEM	PLANNED AMOUNT SPENT PER MONTH
Church	$75
Charity	$50

College Fund for Kids	$300
Roth IRA	$500
Savings (Emergency Fund)	$500
Natural Gas	$50
Water	$162
Mortgage/Rent	$2,000
Electricity	$190
Home Improvement	$200
Taxes	$600 (if you do not escrow)
ADT Alarm Services	$61
Car Gas	$400
Car Maintenance	$50
Groceries	$1,500
Eating Out	$400
Cell Phone Bill	$250
Family Fun!	$250

Hair/Cosmetics	$125
Clothing	$300
Miscellaneous	$100
Pet Care	$200 (2 dogs)
Kids Sports/Activities	$800 (Dance and Baseball)
YouTube TV	$82
Netflix	$22
Amazon Prime	$14
Internet	$105
Doctor Visits/Medical	$100
Life Insurance	$100 (total for 2 adults)
Auto Insurance	$208
Homeowners Insurance	$182
Student Loan (6% Interest Rate)	$200
Visa (21% Interest Rate)	$250

Discover (18% Interest)	$250
Car Loan (4% Interest Rate)	$600

Total Budget: $10,000

Total Spent: $10,251

Margin: -$251

This budget could allow the family of five to save an emergency fund (or a sinking fund if the emergency fund is fully funded), save for retirement, and save $100 per month for each of their children's future college expenses. That would be great! However, due to too many monthly debt payments on things like a car loan, multiple credit cards, and student loans, just to name a few, this budget is overdrawn by $251 per month.

In this case, this family needs to go back into the budget and find places to lower the amount of spending planned for that month. Or find a way to make more income (or better yet, both). Either way, this budget needs to be at $0. All dollars must be allocated to a certain job, and we cannot plan to spend more money than we make. This will only result in more debt. A debt death spiral if you will!

It's time to make some tough choices. Pay off debt, or save and invest? Eat out less, or cancel YouTube TV and Netflix? In this case, this family should pause investing for the time being and pay off their debt. It doesn't make sense to make 10 percent interest on investments while paying 18 percent in monthly credit card interest at the same time.

Get rid of your debt. Save. Then invest. In that order. In this case, pausing the $500 allocated to the Roth IRA for a short time in order to get out of debt would put the family up $249 at the end of each month and create some margin (money left after all bills and expenses are paid) between their expenses and their income, which is a very good thing to have. Pause saving temporarily, and the family will have another $500 per month to throw at their debt. Further increasing their margin. Oh, and sorry, kids, no more Netflix.

Now let's look at a second budget using the same monthly income of $10,000. The only difference is that this family is debt-free.

Example Family Budget 2: $10,000 Monthly Income - No Consumer Debt Payments (Debt-Free!)

BUDGET ITEM	PLANNED AMOUNT SPENT PER MONTH
Church	$75
Charity	$50
College Fund for Kids	$300
Roth IRA	$500
Savings (Emergency Fund)	$500
Natural Gas	$50
Water	$162
Mortgage/Rent	$2,000
Electricity	$190
Home Improvement	$200
Taxes	$600 (if you do not escrow)
ADT Alarm Services	$61

Car Gas	$400
Car Maintenance	$50
Groceries	$1,500
Eating Out	$400
Cell Phone Bill	$250
Family Fun!	$250
Hair/Cosmetics	$125
Clothing	$300
Miscellaneous	$100
Pet Care	$200 (2 dogs)
Kids Sports/Activities	$800 (Dance and Baseball)
YouTube TV	$82
Netflix	$22
Amazon Prime	$14
Internet	$105
Doctor Visits/Medical	$100

Life Insurance	$100 (total for 2 adults)
Auto Insurance	$208
Homeowners Insurance	$182

Total Budget: $10,000

Total Spent: $8,951

Margin: +$1,049

What a difference debt makes! This budget is for the same family with the same monthly income, and this time they are left with $1,300 more each month to save and invest than in Example 1 (the difference between $1,049 and -$251).

Now imagine that $1,300 is invested month after month, year after year, and multiplied over thirty years of compound interest: We are talking about millions of dollars here! In the end, Example 2 is a family of millionaires, and Example 1 is a family living paycheck to paycheck and they both make the same amount of money per month! The only difference is debt (or the lack thereof).

Please remember two things in the big picture here.

One, this family would never have been able to see this incredible difference in outcomes up front, before they happened, and had the chance to course correct and change their future without a budget in place. Remember what I was saying earlier about knowledge giving us the power to see the future? And two, it's not how much money you make; it's how much you can keep. The goal is to become and remain debt-free, and the fastest way to get there is through a monthly budget.

See, I told you this would be fun!

One Last Thought: When I was a kid, my mom used what she called "the envelope system" to save money for expenses like birthdays and vacations, and cars, and Christmas (remember, Christmas is not an emergency when we know it is coming).

Each month she would put money into little white envelopes, each labeled for a cause, and put them in a folder inside of her desk. Then, when it came time to use some of that money, she would open the desk drawer, take it from the designated envelope, and pay the expense. No credit cards. No debt. No stress.

Flash forward to today, and we have automated our

banking systems to the point where we can do this too, only electronically using auto-withdrawals from our checking accounts each month. All we have to do is set up as many savings accounts (virtual little white envelopes) as we would like, label them for a purpose, and have a pre-selected amount of money automatically deposited into those accounts each month from our checking accounts where our paychecks are deposited.

Imagine this: a savings account used only for buying a car someday when needed (a sinking fund if you will), a vacation account, a giving account, a Christmas account, and all of them automatically receiving money each month from your checking account. Then, when the time comes to buy a new car, you take the money out and you buy it with cash. Done. Or when Christmas comes around, you pay the first $1,200 towards Christmas presents without using your regular monthly budget ($100 deposited per month). Or when someone needs help, you are prepared to help them. You literally saved for that purpose. No need to pay it back. It's a gift. It's done.

I know that may seem like a stretch and that there is only so much money to go around, but I also heard an incredible statistic recently that said over 40 percent of Americans went into debt this past year paying for Christmas presents and keeping up with the demands of the holidays. How many of them do you think had a Christmas fund? It's something to think about.

BIG OVERARCHING BUDGETING GOAL:

Set and stick to a monthly budget this month! If you are married, this must be done together and agreed to! You have to be on the same page with your goals or it just won't work. If you are single, set a goal and stick to it. Budgets are for people who have money and want to keep it, not the other way around. Remember that.

Lesson 2

START SAVING AND INVESTING RIGHT NOW. I PROMISE YOU, IT'S TIME.

"The best time to start saving was twenty years ago. The second best time is now."

- Chinese Proverb

"Small amounts saved daily, add up to huge investments in the end."

- Margo Vader

"A penny saved is a penny earned."

- Benjamin Franklin

LESSON 2

However old you are, whatever job you have, however the stock market is performing or not performing, start saving and investing right now. I promise you, it's time.

I had my first job when I was fifteen years old. I woke up one morning, and my dad slipped an application (already filled out) under my bedroom door and said, "Dress nicely for your interview." I was like "Huh?" One week later I was standing in a new black tuxedo with a clip-on bow tie that smelled like butter. That was the way it was back then.

I worked in the concession stand at Marcus Theater in Orland Park, Illinois, and made minimum wage. $5.35 per hour to serve movie theater snacks. Popcorn, nachos with cheese, extra large fountain pops filled with ice, boxed candy, you name it. I was on my way.

Little did I know that the new Star Wars movies were coming out and the theater was about to be packed with people. I have still to this day never seen so many long lines of people waiting to buy tickets, waiting to buy popcorn, waiting for the bathroom, and waiting behind the ropes, in long lines along the theater walls or sitting in circles talking with friends, just to be the first ones let in. It was truly the golden age of going to the movies, and looking back, I guess that's why they were hiring.

I didn't mind too much, because my friends and I loved movies (we still do), and we got to see all of the new movies for free. Even better, we had endless snacks. Some that weren't even on the menu, like pretzel bites and nachos with cheese mixed together in large Diet Coke cups with extra salt. Endless hot, fresh popcorn coming directly out of the poppers. And don't get me started on the fountain Cokes and Sprites.

Now $5.35 per hour doesn't seem like much (minimum wage has nearly tripled now to around $15 per hour), but if I worked fifteen hours a week, I would make about $80. So let's say $320 per month before taxes ($80 x four weeks per month) and $215 after taxes to be safe. Not bad. Now, again, $215 still isn't much, but to me, in 1998, it was.

Now it was that moment, right there when I got that first paycheck, that was the time to start saving. But what did I actually do? I spent it all. Every last cent—and on what, I have no idea. My friends and I went to the mall a lot. Rented movies from Blockbuster Video (look it up, kids, it was a real thing). Rode our bikes to local pizza shops. Collected baseball cards in giant binders with plastic sleeves. Life was good.

What I should have done was set a simple budget, saved some money, and begun investing in a mutual fund. Or helped my parents contribute to my college fund (assuming I had one). All I needed was one of my parents to set up an account and put the money in for me since I was under the age of eighteen. These days, it's easier than ever. Money can be invested in seconds using apps on our phones, and stocks can be bought and sold with the click of a button.

However back then, saving could have been as simple as spending $150 per month (70 percent) on fun and food and movies and nonsense, saving $32 per month

(15 percent) to have a bit of cash in the bank, and investing $32 (15 percent) into an index fund like the S&P 500 and watching my money grow. Heard of the book *Think and Grow Rich?* Well, I was fifteen years old, and all I had to do was hang out with my friends and watch movies and grow rich, as long as I invested 15 percent of my checks each month. I just didn't know it.

If I had done that simple thing, that $32 per month invested would still be making money today over twenty-five years later. Regardless of politics or good or bad growth days (or years) in the stock market, it was an index fund, and it was going up. Way up!

Considering the "Rule of 72" (a simple formula that estimates how long it will take for an investment to double in value), that $32 per month would have been a lot of money today 25 years later. But, who knew?

Let's say that I invested $5,000 total after all of my high school earnings over the years and saved and spent the rest. That $5,000 would have doubled now a little over three times based on the "Rule of 72". The rule is to divide 72 by the expected annual rate of return, which at 10% for example, would double your money on average every 7 years (72/10=7.2). That's doubling your money every seven years on average from age eighteen to age forty! From $5,000 to $10,000 initially, then from $10,000 to $20,000, and again a third time from $20,000 to a little over $40,000!

What seemed like a couple of bucks here and there would be worth over $40,000 today, a little over twenty-five years later! Wait a few more years, and it would have doubled again to $80,000, and that is without investing a single new dollar since high school. Now tell me that isn't fun!

Instead, I spent all of the money on candy and baseball cards and mini tacos (don't get me wrong, it was very important stuff at the time and who doesn't like mini tacos), but now it's all gone!

Now if that story isn't a metaphor for what can happen in your real life if you aren't careful and don't save and invest regularly as the years go on, I don't know what is.

The good news is that $32 is also a very small amount of money compared to the amount you are making now or will be making (and saving and investing) once you graduate college or go into the trades or the military or do whatever it is you choose to do with your life.

The point is, whatever your age, whatever amount of money you are making right now, however big or small, it doesn't matter: start saving 15 percent and investing 15 percent of your income today. Right now, from your next paycheck on, and don't ever look back.

You do that alone and you will have taken a big step towards not only remaining debt-free now (saving), but also building wealth for your future (investing), and that is a very big deal.

BIG OVERARCHING SAVINGS GOAL:

Save at least three months of living expenses, should you ever need it. This money will help safeguard you from any of the unexpected expenses or surprises that come up in life and put so many people into credit card debt. Of course, losing a job would be a big issue for nearly all of us whether we are living paycheck to paycheck or not, but for many, so would needing to replace a kitchen appliance, pay for a car repair, or fix the air conditioner in the heat of the summer. Things are going to happen in life, and your savings will keep you on budget and shield you from going into debt when they do. Because you have a budget now, right?

Lesson 3

BEGIN INVESTING LONG-TERM FOR YOUR RETIREMENT. LIKE RIGHT NOW.

"Earning a lot of money is not the key to prosperity. How you handle it is."

- Dave Ramsey

"If you don't find a way to make money while you sleep you will work until you die."

- Warren Buffett

LESSON 3

O nce you have a full-time job, it's time to set up and begin to fund a long-term savings account for your retirement. The type of account depends on what type of job you have, but there is definitely an account for everyone (403b, 401k, Traditional IRA, Roth IRA, Spousal IRA, and Money Market accounts, to name a few).

Non-profit organizations and government employees like teachers and nurses will invest in retirement using a 403b. Private for-profit company employees will invest using a 401k. Both retirement accounts are very similar; for the most part, it just depends on your career path. In addition to the workplace retirement fund, I highly recommend that everyone opens a second retirement fund as soon as possible, their own personal Roth IRA.

The cool thing about a Roth IRA is that the money is invested directly from your bank account "after tax," so 100 percent of the money in a Roth IRA can be taken out after age fifty-nine and a half TAX FREE! Unlike a 403b or 401k that grows pre-tax and will be taxed upon withdrawal of the money throughout retirement, with a Roth IRA, you get it all! In addition, there are no yearly minimum contributions that you have to put in (there is a maximum of $7,000 per year at the time of writing this), and if you ever truly need the money, your contributions (not earnings) can be taken out at any time without penalty. In other words, that just means that any money you put in can always be taken back out. While that definitely wouldn't be the plan, that kind of flexibility creates a pretty awesome, low-risk retirement fund!

Now it sounds silly, but be sure to buy shares of index funds like the S&P 500 or ETFs that mirror the S&P 500 like VOO (from Fidelity) from inside your retirement accounts each month once they are funded. That is big, and I want to be sure you understand that point. Funding a retirement account isn't investing, and that money will not grow in the stock market. That step just gets the money from your checking account into your retirement account. You then have to take that money and purchase a mutual fund or index fund within your Roth IRA (like the S&P 500 for example) for your money to be invested in the stock market and begin growing.

It sounds silly, but I have heard of stories where people put their money into their retirement accounts each month, but never actually invested it, only to realize thirty years later that it never grew along with the stock market. The money was still there of course, but it acted more like a traditional savings account all those years and never grew a single dollar. It just sat there. Depending on how much money was put in and for how long, those people could have missed out on millions of dollars of compound interest over their lifetime. Ouch!

Remember our example from earlier where we discussed investing $500 per month from age twenty-five to age sixty-five? That money would be worth around $3 million at the time of retirement. However, if that same $500 per month was accidentally saved from age twenty-five to age sixty-five (and not invested and benefiting from compound interest and the rule of 72), it would only be worth $240,000. I don't know about you, but things aren't getting any cheaper, and I'm thinking we could all use that extra 2.75 million dollars when we retire.

I currently invest $250 twice per month ($500 total) in my personal Roth IRA, and since I am a public school administrator in Illinois, my school district also invests money each month on my behalf into TRS (the Illinois Teacher Retirement System) as a job benefit to the position. Pretty great, right? My wife, Jill, is a public school teacher and she also invests money from her paychecks each month into her personal 403b. If all goes according to plan, we will both have our retirement pensions from the Illinois Teacher Retirement System (TRS) when we retire as well as our personal retirement accounts (my Roth IRA and Jill's 403b). If things go badly and the TRS pension system changes for some reason, we will still have saved our own. In this case, it is better to be safe than sorry.

You can do this. I promise you, however hard it is, it isn't as hard as having no retirement nest egg at age sixty-five and having to continue working until you're seventy-five or eighty years old. Here is the good news: once you have this all set up, you don't have to do anything besides sit back and watch your money grow.

Here's one last important rule of thumb, and it's a big one: Do not at any point sell your stocks and move your money outside of your retirement accounts, regardless of how the stock market is performing in any particular month or in any particular year. Other than in a Roth IRA where contributions (not earnings) can be withdrawn at any time penalty free, this will cause large and unnecessary penalties and taxes in most retirement accounts. You are an investor, and when investing long-term, large swings in stock prices, up or down, don't really matter. We are investing for twenty to thirty years from now, not for tomorrow. Dips in the market only provide "discounts" and "sales" from time to time, and that is how you need to look at it. If all goes well, you aren't taking this money out until you retire, which for most, is at least age fifty-nine and a half years old.

UNDERSTANDING THE RULE OF 72: THE 7-YEAR RULE OF INVESTING

Again, this rule tells us how long on average it will take for your investments to double in value. You divide 72 by the average annual rate of return over those years, and that is how long it will take. With a 10 percent annual return (the stock market average over the last one hundred years), it would take 7.2 years on average for your investments to double in value (72/10=7.2).

If you have $20,000 invested when you are twenty years old, and never put in another dime, that money will grow to around $40,000 by the time you are twenty-seven, assuming the average annual return of 10 percent. Then, $80,000 when you are thirty-four years old (after another seven years), and again to $160,000 when you are forty-one, $320,000 when you are forty-eight, $640,000 when you are fifty-five, and $1,280,000 (over 1.25 MILLION DOLLARS) when you are sixty-two, and you are ready to retire.

In this example, you will be a millionaire by age sixty-two! A multi-millionaire by age sixty-nine, and so on. That's compound interest! If you invest when you're young, you will have millions of dollars when you retire, and your wealth will continue to grow as you get older, even in the face of inflation. That's just math!

Follow this lesson, and you will retire free from financial worry. You will be a millionaire, and you will continue getting richer as the years go on. And the best part is, just like we discussed earlier, anyone can do it! So do it! How's that for seeing the future?

A WORD ON INVESTING YOUNG AND INVESTING FOR YOUR CHILDREN

I want you to hear this in all seriousness. If you begin investing $200 per month for your children from the time they are born, at 10 percent average annual growth in a mutual fund like the S&P 500, they will have over 1 MILLION dollars invested on their fortieth birthday. And that $200 per month over that time (480 months X 200 dollars) will cost you only $96,000 of your own money. Compound annual interest and time do the rest and will multiply your money over ten times on average. Incredible.

However, if you start at age fifteen, it will take a little over $800 per month at 10 percent average annual growth for them to become a millionaire on their fortieth birthday (up from $200 per month). If you start at age twenty, it will take $1,500 per month. Almost twice the monthly investment is needed just for waiting five more years.

That's how important starting to invest as soon as you

can really is. Begin with a few dollars each paycheck if you are lucky enough to learn this lesson while you are young. However, begin now, whatever your age. The math doesn't lie. If you listen to one lesson in this book, please listen to this. Invest whatever you can, as soon and as often and as young as you can, and one day long from now it will hit you. Your vision will clear, and you will realize that doing this one simple thing, years and years ago, changed your life and your family's life, forever.

A WORD ON INVESTING IN CRYPTO

Now I of course realize that cryptocurrency investments like Bitcoin, Dogecoin and XRP are complete long shots. I get it. They are volatile, and they cannot be trusted to be there thirty years from now (or 30 minutes for that matter). My advice, however, is to buy a small amount of crypto in a separate account away from your retirement accounts, just in case it skyrockets someday, and leave it alone. Set it and forget it. Don't invest in it monthly, and don't sell it to make a few bucks in profit that you will lose half of at tax time. Leave it alone and in the case that it goes to $0, oh well, that was likely the most probable outcome anyway. However, if it does "go to the moon" one day, you will be on that rocket ship.

Is this gambling or "prospecting" even? Probably. But again, this is just a side bet to your mainstream retirement investing, and if it does hit big one day, it will hit really big, and if it doesn't it doesn't.

I first bought Dogecoin on Robinhood a few years back, and I made over $30,000 one year buying and selling it as its price swung high and dipped low almost daily. However, tax time came, and I owed a lot more than I would have liked in taxes due to these being considered short-term trades.

In the end, Dogecoin tanked one night after Elon Musk made comments hurting its value on *Saturday Night Live.* It lost most of its value (rug pull from .74 cents down to around .08 to .10 cents, where it then held for a few years). I sold at some point on the way down and kept the difference. This is a pretty typical crypto story, actually, but here comes the interesting part.

Do you know what happened next? A few years later, in late 2024, it ran up to .43 cents again seemingly out of nowhere. That is until it started tanking once again in February of 2025. Unpredictable to say the least. So don't chase it.

Now who knows what will happen next, and *never* invest more than you can afford to lose, but I am telling you from my own experience, having lived through what I did and having learned the easy way and the hard way, my advice would be to buy a small amount of Crypto at a very low price and leave it alone for a very long time. Don't chase the highs and sell the lows, don't sweat the ups and downs and you never know: one day you might just get lucky. Ever heard of Bitcoin?

BIG OVERARCHING INVESTING GOAL:

Invest the amount of money you can afford depending upon your age and income and life situation, no matter how large or small the amount, but do invest, and do it sooner than later. Use your birthday money if you have to. Deliver pizzas, give golf lessons, waitress at night, sell things you don't need, babysit, dogsit. Whatever it takes. You simply cannot get those years back. You only get one shot at maximizing compound interest and turning that money into a retirement fund that can give you and your family a wonderful, worry-free life when it comes time to hang up your spikes or put away your dance shoes. Please listen to this advice, if nothing else. This is a big one.

Lesson 4

CREDIT CARDS BUILD
CREDIT SCORES, AND
DEBT, NOT WEALTH.
IF YOU CAN'T AFFORD TO
PAY CASH FOR IT, YOU
CAN'T AFFORD IT.

"Never spend your money before you have it."

\- Thomas Jefferson

"The most important thing to do if you find yourself in a hole is stop digging."

\- Warren Buffett

"Airline miles, cash back, and reward points are just tricks that banks use to keep you in credit card debt."

–Dave Ramsey

"The borrower is slave to the lender."

\- The Bible, Proverbs 22:7

LESSON 4

Please adopt the following mindset when thinking about opening credit cards: Don't. If you can't afford to pay cash for something, other than your home and car, don't buy it.

I'll say it again LOUDLY for emphasis. Credit cards, zero-percent interest loans, and even HELOCs (a Home Equity Line of Credit) are dangerous and they are debt. Stay away from them at all costs. They will mess up your budgeting and investing (like we discussed in Lessons 1 and 2), and turn your free cash into payments. Mess with credit cards too much and sooner or later they will turn into debt. Mess with a HELOC and things go badly, the bank can take your house, regardless of equity. Remember that.

I know, I know, you are paying your monthly credit card balance to zero each month so that you can get the airline miles. Or, even better, you will charge it now and pay it off later that day so you can get the points. All seems well, smart even, and for a long time it may be. But it only takes one or two unexpected things to happen and suddenly you are behind and making monthly payments, and the debt begins to spiral, and for the foreseeable future you are in trouble and you are paying 21 percent interest each month on your balance. How long do you think it would take before the payments on that 21 percent interest each month becomes more expensive than that "free" flight you are trying to earn or those points you are trying to stack up? Who is paying who now? Do you think that maybe that was the credit card company's plan all along?

We can all agree that with so many millions of Americans in credit card debt today, staying out of debt while using credit cards is a lot easier said than done, and it all begins with statements like, "We're doing it for the cash back," and, "We're getting our miles." Take a look at these statistics from 2024:

- According to Bankrate, 48 percent of American credit card holders had a balance in November 2024.

- Forty-three percent of Americans have missed at least one credit card payment in the past five years.

- Fifty-three percent of Americans have reached their credit card limit.

- Twenty-nine percent of Americans max out their credit cards every month.

- Forty percent of Americans have been in credit card debt for over five years.

- The average American spends $1,506 on their credit card each month.

- Credit card interest rates are some of the highest borrowing costs, averaging above twenty percent.

- The most common reason for credit card debt is an emergency or unexpected expense.

Oh. My. Goodness. That is so scary. Can you even imagine how many millions of people are out there right now working long hours away from their families each day (and night) so that they can make monthly debt payments to faceless credit card corporations who are building skyscrapers and buying sports teams with their hard-earned money?

It makes me mad, and it should make you mad too. Even if you aren't in credit card debt, it should make you mad. Commercials showing smiling kids and happy families playing and laughing together in a field on a sunny day. While, in reality, they are selling you (and your kids) new ways to fall into debt. That stuff is wrong and it makes me sad for humanity.

Don't use credit cards. They are dangerous, and they come offering gifts of points and airline miles and cash back, and they are doing it for a reason. They aren't doing it because it loses them money or because it's the nice thing to do, that's for sure. They are "the house" (a casino gambling reference) and they know that sooner or later they will always win.

Have you ever heard the old saying, "A small leak can sink a great ship?" Well, Benjamin Franklin said that, and I love that quote when thinking about personal finances and monthly expenses, because it's so true! Ever heard of the Titanic? Okay, that probably wasn't a small leak, but you understand the metaphor.

Let's get one thing clear: your bank account is the ship, and no matter how much money you make, you better check for leaks in your budget, and check often.

If you're not careful, a bunch of seemingly "small" and "affordable" monthly payments can add up to a whole lot.

Even those "risk-free," zero-due, zero percent interest loans add up. Wait, I thought they were zero-due? Remember, these loans are still debt, and debt leads to monthly payments, and those payments can eat away at your available income and severely delay your ability to save, invest, and become wealthy before you are ninety years old. Don't get me wrong, being wealthy at ninety is great, because number one, you're alive at ninety, but I think we can all agree that doing it by age forty-five or sixty-five is better.

Unless you can out-earn your spending over an extended period of time (and I'm talking like 30 years), credit cards, mortgages, car payments, school loans, and just too many monthly bills in general, no matter how "small," can wipe out your disposable income (your margin) and will nickel and dime you to death if you let them. So don't let them!

Here is a real-world example of this that might hit home. Amazon Prime, Netflix, Paramount Plus, You-Tube TV, MAX, and Disney Plus (to name a few) are all common TV streaming apps that many of us pay for each month. None of them are very expensive on their own; however, if you add up the cost of a few of them and multiply that amount by twelve, you are easily spending over $1,000 per year ($100 per month x 12 months) on TV streaming apps that you may or may not even use. Small things add up!

Think I'm overreacting with the whole credit card thing? I promise you, I'm not. And I'll prove it to you.

Let's say you buy your first house. Now, I don't know about you, but most people prefer not to sit on the floor while they eat dinner. Or on lawn chairs in the family room when they watch TV. So they go shopping.

Need a kitchen table? Bam—you got it! Fifty bucks a month at zero percent interest for twenty-four months. How bad could it be? It's only fifty bucks. Need a couch and loveseat? Bam! They will be there soon. Only one hundred bucks a month for thirty-six months. How about that new fence? I'm not chasing those dogs around the neighborhood every time they have to go to the bathroom. No worries, the guys will be here next month to put it up! Only $150 a month for thirty-six months. Hosting Thanksgiving or Christmas this year? You just might need a dining room table (and extra food and drinks, so plan for that in your December budget too). Bam—it's on the way at zero percent interest! Just one hundred bucks a month for forty months. How about that old, stained carpet in the living room? Who knows where those stains came from, and I think they had a cat. Ahh-choo! That thing should probably be replaced. It's nasty, and our babies crawl on that carpet every day. Done! One hundred bucks a month. Need a new TV? Sure thing! Only seventy-five dollars a month, and if you open a new Best Buy credit card, you can have zero percent interest for twenty-four months!

I can keep going. This is not made up, and it's not uncommon. Businesses thrive all day long and become filthy rich doing this to young families.

Ever watch TV during a holiday like Labor Day or Memorial Day? EVERYTHING MUST GO! ZERO PERCENT FINANCING AND NO PAYMENTS FOR TEN YEARS! HURRY IN, TIME IS RUNNING OUT! To some extent, Jill and I did this when we were first married, and we spent more than a few years paying for it. Pun intended!

It was really easy to do, and the salesmen were super helpful. Lucky us! They must have mistakenly forgotten to mention that if you don't pay off the loans in full by the given timeframes, then you owe all the interest from day one at a very high interest rate.

I'm sure they also just forgot to ever send us a monthly bill in the mail. We certainly never got one. Gone paperless, you say? Oh right, we're all just doing our part to save the environment. That couldn't have been the company's plan all along, right?

Avoid this like the plague! Looking back, would a couple of lawn chairs have been so bad for a few months while we saved enough money to pay cash for a couch? Would our patio set in the dining room all winter with a tablecloth over it have been so horrible after all?

We were so young. Would our parents and friends and those we must have felt the need to impress so badly have even cared at all? Or would they have actually understood and, dare I say, maybe even been a little proud? With the right mindset and goals set between Jill and I, could it even have been a little... fun?

It's not forever, and, in our case, we were just kids. You know what is really fun? Being debt-free. That is fun. Paying for things in cash is fun.

Save and pay cash. Save and pay cash. Save and pay cash. Adopt this mindset: if you can't pay cash for it, you can't afford it. Yet.

Now if my math is correct, those new "no monthly payments" actually added up to about $550 per month. That's $550 less per month, $6,600 less per year, that we had in this example to save and invest in our futures, and we all now know from Lessons 2 and 3 that nothing, short of winning the lottery, or an unexpected inheritance, makes money like compound interest on investments over time. Pay yourself first and don't let anything get in your way.

I'm telling you: no credit cards. They are designed by very smart people sitting around in very expensive board rooms on very expensive chairs (that you paid for), dreaming up ways to keep you paying minimum payments and living paycheck to paycheck, FOREVER. Paying for things months (or even years) after you bought them.

Have you ever made a large credit card payment and couldn't even remember what you were paying for? I know I have, and it sucks. I can't freaking stand it. What kind of financial plan is that? It's not the get-rich-while-you're-young plan, I can tell you that. That "extra" couple hundred (or thousand) dollars per month could be so much better spent! Or saved! Or invested!

BIG OVERARCHING CREDIT CARD GOAL

Life is expensive, and, as you can see, it can leave you pretty much broke if you let it. So don't let it! It doesn't have to be that way. When we know better we do better, and now you know better. You can be smarter than the rest! Smarter than I was when I was young, and smarter than your friends are now. I can promise you this: it's not how much money you make, my friends, it's how much money you can keep and what you do with it that will count in the end. Live a debt-free life and pay for things with cash. You won't regret it.

Lesson 5

LARGE MONTHLY CAR PAYMENTS DON'T MAKE MILLIONAIRES. PAY YOURSELF, NOT THE BANK.

"The best car for you is always the car you can afford to pay cash for."

- Dave Ramsey

"When people don't waste money trying to look wealthy, they have the money to actually become wealthy."

- Dave Ramsey

LESSON 5

Have you ever heard someone say, "Don't go broke trying to look rich?" Well, if you have, that person was smart and they were telling you the truth, so you might want to call and thank them.

Buying a car is a big financial move and, next to your house, it's often one of the biggest financial decisions you will make. So take it seriously. A car can put you into debt faster than almost anything out there.

I get it. Cars are awesome. And new cars are even awesomer (yes, that is a real word believe it or not). They have the latest technology and newest models and the largest moonroofs. They have Wi-Fi so the kid's iPads work on road trips and everything is right with the world. They even smell new, and who doesn't love that? However, we have to remember that, for many people, new cars equal new debt.

More debt and more monthly payments for longer periods of time than necessary. And debt, my friends, is the enemy of wealth. Did you know that the average car payment in the U.S. in 2025 is now up to around $750 per month? That is a lot of tied up cash! I like new cars too, but not that much.

We all know that cars depreciate in value over time and, simply put, just aren't good investments. Did you know that a new car loses 20 percent of its value on average the moment it is purchased and leaves the lot? If you bought a $50,000 brand-new car, it would be worth $10,000 less by the time you got it home. It then continues to lose a significant amount of value each year for the next four years, totaling a 40 percent loss in value on average during that time. After 4 years of payments, that $50,000 car would be worth around $30,000 depending on the make, model and mileage. And many people are now paying $750 per month to a car dealership (or a bank) to let them do it. Think about that.

Have I mentioned Jill and I bought one? We made this mistake in our early thirties, and at that time I honestly didn't know any better. I now have a used car too, and I thought it would be fun for us to compare the two deals.

Our "new" car is a Volkswagen Atlas that we purchased in 2019 and were fortunate enough to pay off in full a few years early in 2023. It has three rows of seating for the kids and tons of room for road trips to Florida which we take as often as we can. It's great. The kids (and Jill) go to sleep and I drive all night and they wake up at the Waffle House in Florida. We really do love it.

But the cost of that new car was around $45,000 out the door after taxes and fees. We put $5,000 down, which was far too little (20 percent down is the general rule of thumb, if not paying for the car in full with cash) and left with a $40,000 car loan. That's $40,000 in new debt!

In other words, we now had the privilege of paying $600 per month for the next six years. Six hundred dollars per month for the next seventy-two months of our lives was gone! Just like that. That's a lot of money we should have been investing and that was a big mistake. Our daughter Bella was eight years old at the time, and when we paid that darn thing off (early, mind you), she was a teenager! Good lord, that's a lot of tied-up cash for a very long time!

Unfortunately, society tells us that this is normal, that it's just what you do when you need to buy a car. It's what you see the happy families doing on the commercials, and it's only getting worse. With rising car prices and smaller down payments, I have heard people have begun signing up for ninety-six-month loans (eight years). Scary.

In comparison, you can get a very reliable, three-year-old "used" car with fifteen to twenty thousand miles on it for fifteen to twenty thousand dollars less than the sticker price, and this, my friends, is the way to do business.

These are still nice, reliable cars. A few years ago I picked up a used, fully loaded Ford Explorer Limited with 14,000 miles on it for $31,000 (still far too expensive looking back, but it's what I did). That SUV had everything. Heated leather seats, cooled seats, dual sunroof, navigation, all-wheel drive, Wi-Fi, you name it. Look it up: that exact SUV was priced at over $50,000 new. I got it for $31,000 because it had 14,000 miles on it and was two years old.

We put $12,000 down and walked out with a $20,000 car loan after taxes and fees. My payment is $375 per month, and we are overpaying it just a bit at $400. At this rate, it will be paid off in four years.

Both cars are very nice, the Atlas and the Explorer, in fact, nicer than we really need. One car was just nearly $20,000 cheaper. We could easily apply the same example to much more affordable, lower-priced cars with higher mileage and come in at lower rates, for fewer months, or even better, just save and pay cash, but the concept remains the same. Most millionaires buy this way until they become millionaires. They buy very nice, reliable, *used* cars until the time comes that they no longer need to.

It is smart financial decisions like this, spread out over many years and in many different situations, that likely allowed them to become millionaires in the first place. I truly believe that.

Also, never lease. I mean, do what you want, but I'm telling you, millionaires don't lease. You will always have a payment, or two, (like always, as in forever) and you will never have a backup emergency fund (other than the one you have saved) if "life happens" and you are in a pickle and need money one day.

What I mean by that is that even though cars depreciate in value and are not good investments, a paid-off car can be sold. Depending on the car, that could be $15,000 to $20,000 cash in your pocket if you ever really need it.

Ask yourself this: if one day you woke up and you truly needed the money, how much can you sell your leased car back to the dealer for after paying $500 per month ($800 to $1,000 per month if you are leasing two) for thirty-six months straight? Nothing. You can sell it back to them for nothing. Zero dollars and zero cents. If you are lucky, the dealer will say that your loan to value has evened out and you can give it back to them for free and go home. That is assuming you didn't go over in miles. If you did that, you will be paying them to give it back!

BIG OVERARCHING CAR BUYING GOAL

My advice to you: go as long as you can without buying a car, save monthly during that time (make monthly payments to yourself), and when you do, buy it "gently used," with low miles and pay cash. A few years old and a few thousand miles never hurt anyone. Let someone else pay the "new car smell" tax. You're too smart for that now.

Lesson 6

~~

FIFTEEN-YEAR HOME MORTGAGES OR NOTHING. NO EXCEPTIONS. THIS IS A BIG ONE.

"Thirty-year mortgages are for people who enjoy slavery so much they want to extend it for fifteen more years and pay thousands of dollars more for the privilege."

–Dave Ramsey

LESSON 6

P lease adopt the following mindset when looking for a house: if you can't afford a fifteen-year mortgage, you can't afford the house. Keep looking.

Buying the right house with the right loan could very well be one of the most important financial decisions you make in your lifetime. And it is very likely one of the most expensive things you will ever buy. So stay true to yourself and your goals here and don't mess them up trying to keep up with the Joneses! Believe me, those neighbors down the street with the huge house and new cars and RV in the driveway may have a lot less money in their bank accounts than you might think.

I bought my first house when I was twenty-four years old. And like everybody else I ever heard of, I got a thirty-year mortgage and didn't think twice. I thought it was "normal," and if I had never seen or heard of anything different, why wouldn't I? In fact, taking a thirty-year mortgage is normal. It's the most common type of mortgage loan, it's what most of our parents likely had at least starting out, and it's what is on all of the commercials that we see on TV (hmm I wonder why?). But that doesn't mean it's the right thing to do!

Had Jill and I gotten a fifteen-year mortgage originally, which we didn't (let me be clear), our house would be paid off now. I would have been forty-two years old with a $450,000 house paid off free and clear (one down the block just sold for $500,000, so you never know). It would have been all ours. No monthly payments. No bank loans. Ours. And it wouldn't have taken a winning lottery ticket or a superpower to do it. Like I said before, just planning, a steadfast commitment to our long-term goals, and time. That's it.

Instead, we got a thirty-year mortgage originally, refinanced twice along the way (first to a 15-year mortgage and later to a 10-year at a historically low interest rate of 2.3%), and now sixteen years later we are on track to pay off our house in just under 4 more years. That tells me we could have done better had we known more about how mortgages work in our twenties. The great news however is that we learned a lot along the way and are currently on track to pay off our original thirty-year mortgage after twenty total years. That's ten years ahead of our original thirty-year payment schedule!

Now, it could definitely be worse. Many people are on a much longer road to having their homes paid off than four years, and for many reasons, I'm thankful, but don't do what we did!

Even though Jill and I were lucky enough to lock in at an incredibly low interest rate of 2.3%, moving from a thirty-year loan to a fifteen-year loan, and later to a ten, we will still have a mortgage for about twenty years total before paying it off in full. Compared to a fifteen-year loan, that's an extra five years of payments (sixty additional house payments), just because we were young and didn't really know any better.

The only way we can beat that now is to make extra payments or overpay monthly on the ten-year loan, which would not necessarily be the smartest move, considering the low interest rate we currently have. If we had any debt at all outside of the mortgage, we would be better off paying the extra hundred or two per month toward those debts and not the house, because those interest rates (from credit cards) would likely be much higher than 2.3 percent. Remember what we said earlier? The average credit card interest rate is now over 20 percent.

Live within your means and stay focused on making the correct financial decision here. This is a big one, and a fifteen-year mortgage will put you on a great path towards the kind of financial freedom and peace that comes with being debt-free, and we didn't even get into how much less money you will pay over the life of the loan in interest (A LOT LESS). Buy the house, start a family, have a great life, and put in the pool if you have saved up for it and are debt-free, just do it with a fifteen-year mortgage!

BIG OVERARCHING MORTGAGE GOAL:

The plan here is simple. Get a fifteen-year loan and pay the house off as soon as you can. The sooner the better. It is most likely the largest monthly bill draining your bank account each month, and you need that money to invest. Then simply take the extra couple thousand dollars that you were paying on the mortgage every month and accelerate your investing. That is the road to wealth.

Or, split the difference and go for life balance (the Yin and Yang and the Y.O.L.O. in all of this). Let's say you're now up $2,000 a month with no mortgage to pay. Keep $1,000 a month and live well. You were smart. You planned for this, and you patiently waited fifteen years for that plan to pay off. It will feel like you got a huge raise because you did (+$24,000 net per year), and you deserve it. Take care of your family, go on vacation, and bump up the college savings funds for the kids. Do whatever you want. Then take the other $1,000 per month and invest it in a money market account or accelerate your retirement fund (that you already have, remember?). It's a win-win!

Lesson 7

OPEN A 529 COLLEGE SAVINGS PLAN FOR EACH OF YOUR KIDS AND BEGIN FUNDING THEM MONTHLY. NO MATTER HOW SMALL THE AMOUNT.

"The habit of saving is itself an education."

\- TT Munger

"An investment in knowledge
always pays the best interest."

\- Benjamin Franklin

LESSON 7

THIS IS NOT A DRILL. Open a 529 college savings fund for each of your kids. I can't say it any more straightforward than that, and I don't care if you think you have plenty of time because college is eighteen years away and you can do it next year, or if you think you don't have enough money right now to make the payments. I promise you, open the savings accounts for your kids and start funding them, no matter how small the amount. Like the day after they are born.

So what is it? A 529 is a tax-advantaged savings plan that helps parents save for their kids' college tuition and other educational expenses. In other words, it is money that you invest today that grows in the stock market and can be used to pay for your children's college expenses when the time comes. This would of course include tuition first and foremost, but also room and board, books for their classes, tech needed for school like a laptop, school supplies, apprenticeships if going into the trades, and even loan repayment if loans are still needed outside of what is saved in the 529 when the time comes.

There are a few helpful tax advantages for parents to be aware of as well. Funds can be withdrawn tax-free when using them for educational expenses, and up to $20,000 can be deducted each year from your taxable income when filing taxes jointly in Illinois ($10,000 if filing individually). That's always a good thing. Less taxable income can bring your tax bracket down, and that means more money in your pocket at tax time.

College is so expensive these days, and the price is only going up. Heck, everything is so expensive these days. We need every advantage we can get, and nobody wants their children coming out of college after four or five years with six figures in student loan debt. Nobody.

Do you have any idea how long it would take a young family to pay off $100,000 in loan debt? If they paid two hundred dollars per month every month and never missed a payment, depending on the interest rate, it would take around forty years on average to pay off in full. Forty years of payments for going to school! At that rate, if they graduated from college at twenty-three years old, they would be sixty-three years old when the loan was finally paid in full. They would likely be retired!

Now I understand that loan forgiveness is out there, but most loans aren't actually forgiven, and even if they *might* someday be forgiven ten years into payments, that's still no way to plan. Imagine saying this to your children: "Here is the plan, kids. If you do your best and graduate from college and get a good job and make 120 on-time payments of two hundred dollars or more per month for ten straight years, we can then ask the government for loan forgiveness, and they will let us know if you qualify." No, thank you. And just to throw it out there, declaring bankruptcy isn't an option if things go bad, because student loans aren't "bankruptable" (I don't think that is technically a word but it should be). Meaning that under current law, you can't get rid of student loan debt by declaring bankruptcy.

Saving for college is such an important topic right now that many states are now even stepping in and trying to do it for us themselves by providing a small "seed fund" for babies that are born after 2023. All the parents need to do is open a free 529 college savings account and make an initial investment. Illinois, for example, has a program through Bright Start (their 529 savings plan holders) that gives parents the first fifty dollar seed investment in the child's college savings account as an incentive for opening it. It's called Illinois First Steps and can be found at Brightstart.com. Even if no other payments are made, that $50 will grow in the stock market for 18 years and that child will have a bit of money to start out with in college.

If all you do when your child is born is open that account, match the fifty dollar gift from First Steps, and start with that initial investment of one hundred dollars invested in a mutual fund ($50 from First Steps and $50 from the parents), you will be off to a great start. That alone would be more than what most people do and it would be happening far sooner.

Then, if for example you take the next big step and invest fifty dollars per month (set up automated payments) until your son or daughter enters college at the age of eighteen, you will have a good amount of money in there for them to get started.

Since 529 funds are invested in index funds like the S&P 500, that investment of fifty dollars per month would be worth upwards of $29,000 at the time your son or daughter enters college, again assuming an average annual return of 10 percent for eighteen years. Now, yes, college costs more than $29,000, but it is so much better than zero dollars, and the best part is that you would have only invested $10,900 of that $29,000 in your own money and it would have nearly tripled over the years invested! Compound interest strikes again!

Now, just for the heck of it, let's say you put in one hundred dollars per month for eighteen years instead of fifty dollars. That fund would have an estimated $58,000 in it after eighteen years! Two hundred dollars per month invested for eighteen years would be over $115,000, and so on. Now we're talking.

The more you invest monthly and the sooner that you start investing, the more money that will be there for your son(s) or daughter(s) when they need it. And it won't have to come out of your paycheck and budget at the time. To me, that's not just money, that's peace of mind. I mean, like I said before, I have three kids, and they were all born within two years of each other (the twin factor). Fast forward eighteen years, and that means all three of them will enter college someday, God willing, at roughly the same time. How could Jill and I afford that if we didn't save and take advantage of compound interest?

Now, what if you waited a few years to begin investing? Let's say you opened a 529 and began saving for your daughter's college expenses when she turned ten years old instead of when she was born. That same two hundred dollars invested through age eighteen would be worth somewhere around $30,000, assuming the same 10 percent average rate of return over those years (instead of $115,000 if invested when she was born). That's a big difference but again, regardless of our children's age, we can't go back in time. We can only make the next best decision and keep moving forward.

If you haven't started your kids college fund yet, it's okay. Just don't get stuck there; today is the day then.

Final Thought: Now what if you invest all those years and your kids don't go to college? There are of course other things they may do in life. Trades, military, family business, etc. The good news is that these plans are now extremely flexible. If you have two children and one decides not to go to college, the funds can be transferred to the child who does. Also, the savings funds can now be used to pay for schooling and supplies needed when entering careers in the trades, which is awesome. And, finally, if none of your children use the funds, guess what? You can change the beneficiary to yourself!

BIG OVERARCHING COLLEGE SAVINGS GOAL:

If you have kids and you have not opened their 529 college savings plans please stop reading this and go open those now. All you will need are their social security numbers, their birth dates, and a bank routing and account number to pull the funds from each month. It's a no-brainer, and I promise you, the best day to start saving for your kids' futures is today. So go do it!

Lesson 8

BUY LIFE INSURANCE FOR
YOU AND YOUR SPOUSE
THE MINUTE YOU HAVE A
FAMILY THAT IS COUNTING
ON YOU. TRUST ME.

"Remember, you can't get life insurance once you need it."

- Anonymous

LESSON 8

A strange thing happened when my wife, Jill, and I went to the hospital to deliver our twin boys. We were in our late twenties at the time, and our firstborn daughter, Bella, was at home waiting with Grandma and Papa. She was nearly two years old, and she was so excited to meet her brothers.

It was early June, and I still remember it being warm and sunny outside that day. I remember watering the flowers in the backyard together before we left for the hospital and talking casually as we often did.

Jill and I were both young, healthy, and excited about our life ahead. Twins are an incredible gift, and we knew it. Even today, all these years later, I still find it hard to wrap my head around having one child one day and three the next!

With twins, lots of things are like that. The backseat of your car has one car seat and plenty of room one day, and is completely full, door-to-door with car seats the next. The number of cribs in the house tripled. The clothes tripled, and all of the bedrooms filled up. Everything in our lives seemingly tripled overnight and in many ways, it did!

Anyway, we had the rest of our lives with our new family to look forward to and life insurance was the furthest thing on our minds at the time. We were aware that we needed it and thought about it a few times, yes, but as something that we needed to get done at some point when we could find the time. We didn't know much about which type to choose, and appointments and blood work and approvals were just too much to think about at the time. After all, let's be real: we weren't planning on dying anytime soon. But really, who is?

Well, fast forward to the hospital and, like I said, something strange happened when Jill was delivering our boys. Moments after both boys were delivered safely into the world, Jill looked up at me and said that she felt strange and then her eyes began to close, her head tilted to the side, and she was gone.

As it turns out, Jill had a very rare complication during childbirth called an Amniotic Fluid Embolism, more commonly referred to as an AFE. This is when amniotic fluid enters the mother's bloodstream during delivery and causes an anaphylactic shock type reaction often leading to cardiovascular collapse. Now, to be honest, an AFE wasn't just rare, it was exceedingly rare (about 1 in 40,000 deliveries), and we came to understand pretty quickly that it was also absolutely deadly.

As I watched in shock, someone began yelling to the doctors for help (later I realized it was me), machines started beeping loudly, nurses started running, and everyone began talking frantically. I remember an emergency code going over the loudspeaker of the entire hospital. Jill's mom, a pediatric nurse working on another floor at the time, heard this too and came running. She knew what that code meant. Jill's heart had stopped, and she was bleeding internally.

I remember like it was yesterday being in the hallway outside of the delivery room. At some point, one of the doctors came out to tell me that Jill's heart had stopped numerous times and that, so far, she had been brought back to life each time, but that, "It didn't look good." That she was "the sickest person in the hospital right now," and that she "wasn't likely to make it the next hour, and if she did, she wasn't likely to live through the night." Can you imagine?

Well, little did we know a miracle was about to happen. As it turns out, a doctor was in the hospital that day that also worked out of Rush Hospital in Chicago and he too heard the emergency code go out over the hospital loudspeaker. We found out later on that he was the only doctor in the hospital who believed he had seen something like this before, and that he also believed he could save Jill if a certain room was open in the hospital with certain new medical equipment that had just arrived and gone into use.

We now know that when an AFE takes place during childbirth, even today, in 2025, the mortality rate for the mother is 50-80 percent. It just isn't something the medical field has fully figured out. It comes out of nowhere, and it's devastating. A silent killer.

Well, as it turns out, the new medical equipment was there in the hospital that day, the special room housing it was open at the time, and that incredible doctor stepped in and saved Jill's life. As I said, a miracle happened that day, and I truly believe that. But the story doesn't stop there.

Jill was then placed in a medically induced coma so that her body could rest, and again we were told that she was not likely to survive. That she was just too sick and that she may still be bleeding internally somewhere unknown. That first night, our family priest and pastor came and the last rites were given.

Well, she did survive the night. And the next day, and then the next. We were told that she may not wake from the coma and that if she did, extended oxygen loss to the brain during the initial attempts to save Jill's life may have caused irreversible brain damage. Machines were currently helping her breathe, and we just didn't know.

Now during that time, family and friends gathered from all around. For days we prayed and talked to Jill and read books to her. Family came and went, and one day I looked over at Jill in the hospital bed and, would you believe it, she opened her eyes and woke up. Just like that.

Not only did Jill survive, but after a few weeks of recovery, regaining the strength to walk, and regaining her memory, she went home to her three babies and never looked back. To this day she never uses it as an excuse for anything that happens even though we both know that she could.

Soon after, the hospital held a special celebration where we met and thanked the doctors and nurses and the story even made the local newspaper. We still have the article clipping today with our family picture in it. An honest to goodness miracle, and I do believe God stepped in that day and decided it wasn't her time.

I tell you that story for one reason, and I hope it hits home. When we went to the hospital that day, Jill and I didn't have life insurance. Like I said, we were in our 20s and planned to be living for quite some time to say the least. It was just so easy to put off for another day, and, again, we really didn't understand all the options.

However, had things gone differently that day, I would have gone home as a single parent with three babies and one income in a house that was running on two. In the middle of all that sadness and chaos and funeral planning and diaper changing, I would have also been selling our family's home, because there would have been no way to afford it. I just don't see another way that it would have gone.

Well, Jill came home, and in the middle of all the craziness, we learned our lesson and found the time to do the right thing. We made our calls, did our blood work, and added our life insurance policies directly after. That was now twelve years ago, and we have had life insurance every day since and have it in place until each of us reaches age sixty. By then, the hope is we will be our own life insurance (our investments, savings, etc.).

Don't make the mistake we did and put it off for another day because you are young or you are busy or you can't afford it right now. Don't push it off for another hour. I promise you, you never know. If you have a family and you want to be sure they are taken care of if something happens, get life insurance, and get it now. Like today.

BIG OVERARCHING LIFE INSURANCE GOAL:

Get life insurance for both you and your spouse. This cannot be put off. Most people recommend term life insurance because it is the cheapest and most affordable way to get the largest amount of money for your family if, God forbid, it is ever needed. (Ten to twelve times your annual income is the recommended amount of coverage you will need.) At the time, I didn't know any better, and we signed up for what is called Return of Premium Life Insurance. It has its benefits as well; for example, as long as Jill and I live until age sixty, we will receive every cent of our life insurance payments back in a check for $60,000. That is awesome, but it is more expensive month to month for the time of the coverage, and commonly accepted advice is to go with term insurance. It is cheaper, and you can take the difference in the monthly expense and invest it and make your own $60,000, or more if you are disciplined and smart enough to do it.

Either way, do the research, stay away from "whole life" (it's commonly accepted as a bad deal), and get yourself and your spouse life insurance, most likely term, today. You will not regret it, and you will sleep easier knowing your family is taken care of should the unexpected happen. That alone is worth it. I can promise you that.

A life-changing delivery

Woman survives rare, deadly condition after delivering twin boys

BY JEANNE MILLSAP
For the Herald News

JOLIET — Mothers usually have one big prayer during their pregnancy — that nothing goes wrong and their babies are delivered healthy.

That was precisely Jill Wieher's prayer during her pregnancy with twin boys this year, and she was ecstatic it came true. But, immediately after her boys were delivered strong and full of vigor, Wieher collapsed.

"My heart had stopped," she said.

And that was not all. Over the next few hours, she would go into shock, experience disseminated intravascular coagulation (DIC), go into cardiac arrest twice, and receive more than 20 units of blood products.

"The situation was very tenuous," she said.

She was stabilized at Saint Joseph Medical Center. She was very sick for a few days.

"There are not many patients who get out of a situation like Jill's. She had suffered from amniotic fluid embolism, or AFE, a pregnancy-associated condition that has a 61 percent to 80 percent mortality rate."

Both pregnancy

No one had any issues with pregnancy and delivery woes, progressing but normal. Although carrying twins, her pregnancy the year before was without a hitch, and this one, that just as well. She found out she was carrying two after an ultrasound last Halloween.

Jill and Brad Wieher of Joliet with their newborn twins, Michael and Devin, and daughter Isabella. After the twins were born, Jill Wieher suffered a condition called amniotic fluid embolism, which caused her to go into shock and experience cardiac arrest and severe blood loss. A team of 15 healthcare workers saved her life, and she spent 12 days in the hospital recovering. | SUBMITTED PHOTO

him the news. She knew raising the twins along with her young daughter would be a challenge, but she sailed through the pregnancy, delivering at 37 weeks — full term for a multiple pregnancy.

A Caesarean section was scheduled, but after she called her obstetrician with a question about the decreased movement of the babies, she was told to go in and they would deliver a little bit earlier than planned. ... her going in at ...

... twins were delivered, she told him she wasn't feeling right, then she suddenly ... For the next ... life is still a blank memory ...

Tepper recounts that ... he received a call that day from his colleague Dr. Kristopher Mc-Donough, a Provena critical care physician. Tepper said he happened to be in the hospital at the time and the "angio suite" happened to be available.

Wieher was rushed into the suite.

"She was in sh...

a case of AFE before, but he h... handled such severe hemorrha... ing before and knew exactly wh... to do. As far as he knows, the... had never been a case of AFE ... the hospital, either.

It's so rare that it occurs in only one of every 15,000 pregnancies. It's so deadly, though, th... it is the second leading cause ... maternal death. Tepper said t... condition is not well underst... but it's thought to be caused ... an anaphylactic reaction of ... mother's immune system to th... mucin secretions of the baby in... her bloodstream.

"It can be like a poison to some mothers," he said.

Medical teamwork

Tepper's job was to find the source of the bleeding and stop it. There were 15 people in the room, he said, all working to save Wieher's life. By this time, she was in DIC, which Tepper said resulted in the blood not clotting properly.

Several transfusions were given. So too, during that time, Tepper performed an angiogram where he found the source of bleeding in one of the uterine arteries and stopped it.

A team of physicians and staff from anesthesia, surgery, respiratory, cardiology, interventional radiology, the lab and more were involved saving Wieher's life. Mc-Donough was bedside bed for five days.

"The team nailed it," Tepper said. "Everyone did their job, and it all came together with miraculous results."

In the hospital for 12 days, Wieher only remembers the last half. She never recovered ... worrying what might happen to ... during the delivery? She and ... was always just ... the babies, just ...

Wieher is now enjoying ...

Lesson 9

LIFE IS EXPENSIVE AND GETTING MORE EXPENSIVE. FIND A SIDE HUSTLE.

"Never depend on a single income. Make an investment to create a second source."

- Warren Buffett

"The trouble for most people is they don't decide to get wealthy, they just dream about it."

- Michael Masters

"The longer you're not taking action, the more money you're losing."

- Carrie Wilkerson

LESSON 9

S o how do we do all of this budgeting and saving and investing while also living and enjoying our lives? I mean, life is expensive! I don't know what it is, but no matter how much money you make at work, it can all disappear pretty quickly if you aren't careful.

One thing that I have found to help, and actually be a little fun along the way, is a side hustle. Earning a couple of extra bucks on the side, doing something you dreamt up, ideally, something you enjoy doing just for you, feels awesome and can really help. One hundred dollars a week may not sound like much at first, but would an extra four hundred dollars per month help you? That's an extra $4,800 per year!

Making extra money just feels good. Especially if it's

cash. Like finding a twenty dollar bill crumpled up in your jeans pocket. Who doesn't love that? It may only be twenty bucks, but it's exciting!

For me, it has been a few things. Back in my twenties I coached high school baseball. I found out quickly that even the best players could use a bit of work understanding different mental aspects of the game. They needed help staying in the moment, living presently for every pitch, breathing properly, moving on after a bad call, knowing what to do in any given situation, and so on.

So I created what I called "Need to Know Baseball." They were these little slices of paper that I would print and cut out before practice each day, and they were filled with cool baseball fundamentals, tips, strategies, mindset tricks, sayings, famous quotes, and whatever I could find that seemed interesting and relevant to what we were practicing on the field. I read book after book after book and, in the end, made my own.

Then the kids would pick the pieces of paper up from me after practice or on the bus on the way to a game, and we would read and discuss them. It got to the point where if I didn't have time to bring them to practice, the players would ask for them. It was fun, and we all learned a lot.

As time went on, I saw an opportunity and began turning them into short videos and selling them to a baseball company that was adding them to their website. Each month, I would submit a few videos, and bam, cha-ching: money in the bank! It wasn't much, but it was fun! And when I wanted to go to a Cubs game or bet on them to win the World Series (which I did and won in 2016), I took the money from that account. Leaving the family budget untouched. Which was even more fun!

These days, after many years as an educator, I continue to sell a few things here and there on a teaching website. Creating the items and setting up the sales page on the website was the hard part. But you know what? It was fun figuring out how to do it, and even today, ten years later, every once in a while someone pays to download my materials and my phone screams out cha-ching! (Literally; it's my ringtone for that notification!)

I'll be sitting on the couch watching a game or playing with the kids and, bam, cha-ching, eighteen bucks! At the grocery store, and cha-ching, twenty bucks! It only happens a few times a week or so, but it's great! I make money while I'm sleeping, and I even made money at church once! Again, it's not much, but the money automatically deposits into an account at the end of each month, and I now pay my YouTube TV bill with it. That bill rarely hits my family's bank account, and that's really cool. As my friends and I like to say: free money!

Another friend of mine airbrushes incredibly realistic looking fishing lures and sells them at local bait shops on our yearly fishing trip while the rest of us are buying fishing licenses and bait. For you, it may be selling oils or setting up a clothing store on Facebook. I know someone who bakes cakes for birthday parties and never seems to run out of requests. I know a great dad who 3D prints fun things with his two boys and sells them at local craft fairs on the weekends. It doesn't matter what it is. Figure out how to make a few bucks doing something you love on the side. Give a few drum lessons on the weekends. Anything!

Whatever it is, my advice is to make it something you enjoy doing and that doesn't "feel like work." You already have a job. I am willing to bet that if you really think about it, there is something you already enjoy doing that could earn you and your family a few extra bucks each month. All you have to do is try. Don't tell anybody if you don't want to. I rarely do. Then, if it doesn't work out, so what?

Try something else. It's not like you're quitting your day job, and it doesn't have to be anyone else's business. You do you, kid.

BIG OVERARCHING SIDE HUSTLE GOAL:

Find a side hustle that makes you happy and try to work towards bringing in a little extra cash for you and your family. I can promise you one thing: it feels great. Not because you are getting rich off of it (because you probably aren't), but because you did it on your own and the money is helping your family stay on budget and meet your financial goals. It's different. You had an idea, a thought in the air, and you turned that thought into real money in your pocket. Now that's just cool.

Lesson 10

CARRY CASH, BE
GENEROUS, AND STAY
FOCUSED OUT THERE.
MONEY ISN'T MONEY.
IT'S FREEDOM.

"A simple fact that is hard to learn is that the time to save money is when you have some."

- Joe Moore

"Wealth is not about having a lot of money. It is about having a lot of options."

- Chris Rock

LESSON 10

There has always been something about pulling out a stack of cash from your pocket and paying for dinner with it or throwing your kids a twenty dollar bill on their way out with friends. Sending your kids fifteen dollars through Zelle or Apple Pay just isn't the same. It's what I do these days more often than not, but it's not the same.

Today, carrying cash is also once again a smart financial decision. There was a time when I honestly thought the simplicity and convenience of having a debit card in this world would completely take over the need for cash in our pockets, but, honestly, I was wrong.

Have you noticed that more and more restaurants these days, as well as many other places, have even begun charging a 3 percent fee for using credit and debit cards to pay the bill? They don't even tell you about it most of the time. It's just a line item in small print on the bottom of the bill. A convenience fee passed down from the credit card companies to the business owners to us, the consumer.

Instead, plan ahead and take a couple hundred dollars out of the bank when you get paid or at the start of each month and pay certain things with cash. Life is expensive. Save your money. Save the three dollars. It's the principle of the thing.

If nothing else, most of us would rather spend that extra money on a family member, helping a friend, or tossing it in the basket at church. Anything is better than giving it to the credit card companies. Would you let them reach into your pockets and take three dollars because it is only three dollars? Heck no, you wouldn't!

Ever heard the expression, "It's the thought that counts"? A few years ago a good friend of mine unexpectedly sent me five dollars through PayPal on my birthday with a message that said, "Happy birthday, my friend, your first drink is on me." Wow! It cost him five dollars and only a minute or two of his time to do that, and I'll never forget it. What a great idea, and what a cool person for taking the time to do that unexpectedly.

We can all look for more moments like this once we begin to have a bit of cash in our pockets. Pick up the tab for the table from time to time when it's not expected. It could be twenty bucks or one hundred, it doesn't matter. People will remember that and it feels good too.

Remember your family members' and godson's and goddaughter's birthdays and send them a card each year with a little cash in it. Or send them a Happy Birthday text message with $15 bucks in it from Apple Pay and say "Happy Birthday kid, lunch is on me!"

Take your kids and their friends out bowling once in a while and get a pizza or go to the movies and get popcorn and let their friends know that when they are with you no money is needed. Let your kids see that. Give back to your church and your closest friends and your favorite charity, and let your kids see that too. They are watching and little by little they are learning.

Remember, having money isn't the reason to have money. We don't save and invest and build wealth for the sake of saving and investing and building wealth. We do it because money gives us security, and options and it allows us to live the life we want to live. A paid off house means nobody can take your family's home. A paid off car means it's your car, not the banks. Having money saved means nobody can tell you what to do or how to think. If your job no longer has meaning or your boss is a bad person, you quit your job. You're not stuck working someplace because it pays well and you have debt and monthly payments that need to be made. If you need a fresh start and you want to move, you move. If you want to be generous and help a family member or a friend going through a hard time, you help them. If someone in your family is sick, you find them the best doctor on this planet to help them heal. If you want to unplug and spend more time with your kids, you put the phones and the laptops down and you walk away.

If you remember nothing else remember this. Money isn't money. It's freedom.

Best of luck, everyone.
Brad

ABOUT THE AUTHOR

Brad Wieher is a nonfiction author and educator. With Master's degrees in both Literacy and School Leadership, he brings a unique perspective and a sense of urgency to his writing. Brad lives in the Chicago suburbs with his wife Jill, their three teenagers, Isabella, Michael, and Danny, and their two dogs.

For more information about Amniotic Fluid Embolisms and to help #endAFE, visit https://afesupport.org.

To follow the #10ThingsNobodyToldMeAboutMoney journey, Brad can be found on his Instagram author page @bradwieher.writes.

www.ingramcontent.com/pod-product-compliance
Lightning Source LLC
Chambersburg PA
CBHW051321120626
46547CB00015B/2331